Pam and Tom

by Kristin Cashore
illustrated by Bob Brugger

Scott Foresman
is an imprint of

Glenview, Illinois • Boston, Massachusetts • Mesa, Arizona
Shoreview, Minnesota • Upper Saddle River, New Jersey

Every effort has been made to secure permission and provide appropriate credit for photographic material. The publisher deeply regrets any omission and pledges to correct errors called to its attention in subsequent editions.

Unless otherwise acknowledged, all photographs are the property of Pearson.

Photo locations denoted as follows: Top (T), Center (C), Bottom (B), Left (L), Right (R), Background (Bkgd)

Illustrations by Bob Brugger

Photograph 8 ©DK Images

ISBN 13: 978-0-328-39291-9
ISBN 10:   0-328-39291-X

1 2 3 4 5 6 7 8 9 10 V010 17 16 15 14 13 12 11 10 09 08

Tom and little Tip live on a farm.

3

Tom and Tip came from the
farm.
Help! Get us back!

Pam and little Mops live in town.

Pam and Mops came from the town.

Help! Get us back!

Tom and Tip use a blue tractor.

Pam and Mops use a cab.

They like where they live.

Where People Live

Read Together

People live in the city, in the country, in deserts, in the mountains, and in the jungle. People live all over the Earth! Some places have many people. Some places do not have many people.

Where do you live? Do many people live there?

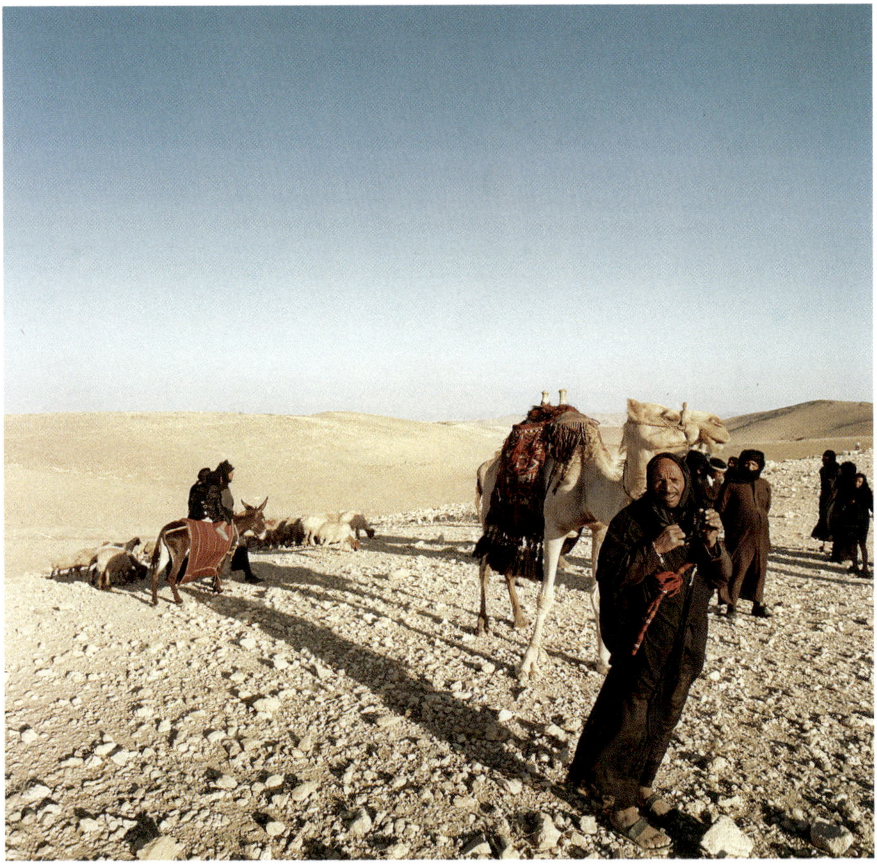